Finding the King of the Corporate Jungle

Finding the King of the Corporate Jungle

A Leadership Fable

Karri T. Perez & Richard S. Colfax

To order additional copies of this book, contact:
Xlibris Corporation
1-888-795-4274
www.Xlibris.com
Orders@Xlibris.com
44410

Contents

Acknowledgements

To both our spouses and children,
Thank You for your encouragement and support.

We also want to thank the University of Guam
and our colleagues at the
School of Business and Public Administration
for their encouragement.

We want to recognize that
the Artwork was contributed
by Professor Ric Castro's Advanced Illustration Students
at the University of Guam:
John San Augustin
Ping-Yung Kuo
Ronald P. Labrador

"May you always look first in the home jungle for talent."

Foreword

Diversity and inclusion—making sure that what we do as leaders is inclusive of everyone's talents and has sustainable, positive results on the communities in which we live.

These are admirable ideals, but sometimes, history and our own comfort level with "doing things the way we've always done them—with people who are from our comfort zone" may keep us, as global business leaders, from maximizing our local human resources. We hear a lot these days about taking care of our natural resources. This will always be a concern, as once they're gone, they're gone for good. But how often have we lost talent only to find out how irreplaceable THAT is? How often have we lost unique opportunities because of lack of talented human resources? This story addresses taking care of our businesses by taking the long-term approach and "growing" our local talent.

This is a short fable about a jungle. It is a story about strategies, and successes and failures, and failures that lead to successes. In short, it is about seeking and finding talented leaders in places (and in people) who we might ordinarily overlook. It is a story about growing your organization globally—and successfully.

Michael McBreen
President, Global Operations Group
Wolverine World Wide

Chapter 1

Opal's Introduction

This is not my story. It's a story of the jungle and the animals that live and lead there. It is a story told by me, Opal, an old owl. I've lived in this jungle of Red all my life and I know everything because I sit in my tree, watch, listen and learn. I only give advice when asked, and that rarely happens.

You may recognize this story and the animals in it because all jungles have these situations in common. Hopefully everyone who aspires to be a leader, or is one now, will learn something from this tale.

This story takes place in the region of Rainbow. Rainbow has three small countries: the jungle countries of Red and Blue which are separated by the desert country of Yellow.

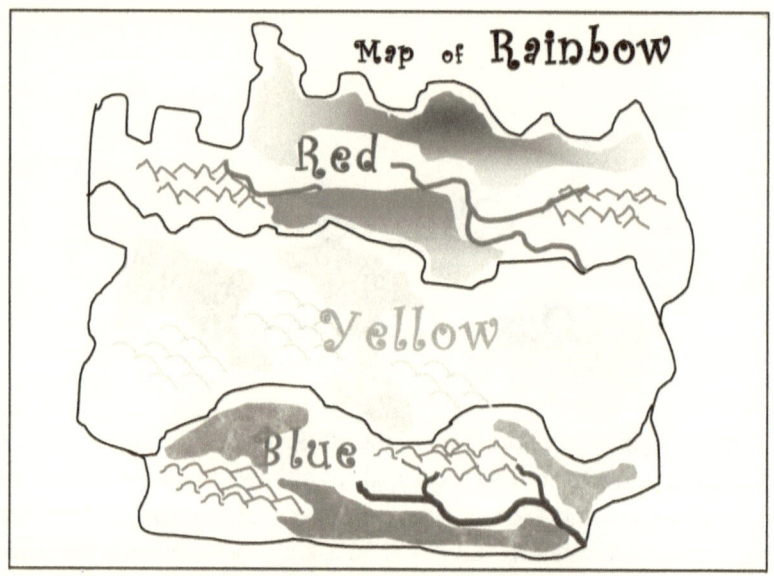

I want to tell you about the jungle of Red and what has happened there in the last few years. In the beginning, Red was ruled for many years by a wonderful lion named Seth . . .

Chapter 2

Seth of Red

Seth, the lion, led Red for many, many years. He'd started as a young cub and I, Opal, watched him grow into a good leader.

He generally chose good advisors from within the community, even if they were not lions. He listened to just about everyone: carnivores, herbivores, and omnivores. He included all sorts of animals on his team. Over the years he listened to the large and the small, the strong and the weak, the young and the old. He included the baboons, giraffes, hyenas, spiders, elephants, zebras, wildebeests, hawks, vultures, alligators, and impala. He listened to me when he was a young leader.

As a young lion, Seth was strong, brave, and smart. Even so, he'd made some mistakes. But because he listened to advice, his mistakes were generally small and not very frequent. He maintained control of the potential troublemakers, including the hyenas and jackals. He kept them all in line, even Hector the hyena, their leader and the biggest troublemaker. Seth was respected, not feared, by the animals of Red.

As he got older, Seth became tired and less enthusiastic as a leader. He did not pay such close attention to all the details as he once had. The jungle of Red deteriorated. The animals did not want to cooperate with each other. Some took off on their own while others tried to create exclusive little kingdoms independent of all others.

Seth's hold on his reign began to crumble and he stopped talking to his advisors and stopped listening to the animal community. He withdrew from actively leading Red and let things go their own way. Rumors began to surface about many different things. Some were true, some were not. Animals even began to whisper about Seth's health and ability to lead.

Finally some animals sent word to Rainbow headquarters about the situation in Red. Adam was summoned . . .

Chapter 3

Adam arrives from Rainbow

Adam was the leader in charge of Rainbow. As the top leader, he was responsible for making sure that local leaders like Seth were doing their jobs. Getting reports on the performance of different jungle leaders was a regular part of his job. When there were problems, Adam had to take action.

Adam came to Red to see what was happening. He listened to the different animals and their complaints about Seth's recent performance. He also spent some time observing how things were going on in Red. It became apparent that a change was needed.

When Adam had been a young lion cub in Red, he had reported to Seth. Seth had taught Adam how to be a good leader and Adam had gone on to take charge of Rainbow. Now Adam had the sad job of removing Seth from his position as leader of Red.

I, Opal, wondered how Adam was going to do this. How was he going to tell his mentor that it was now time for him to step down or be removed? And I wondered how Adam would deal with the hyenas and jackals and other carrion eaters who would try to take Seth's position of power for themselves?

Adam lost a lot of sleep over this decision when he returned to Red. I should know, as I watched him every night he was there. But he knew it had to be done because Seth had lost his leadership touch. Red was in a state of chaos.

Since Seth had once mentored Adam, he should have been very proud of Adam's approach to the situation. Adam took Seth aside and talked to him as the respected elder he was. He explained to Seth that

Red needed a strong hand to lead and guide it into the next era. He explained that Seth had served Red well and deserved a rest.

Seth was grateful and maintained his dignity, gracefully announcing he would retire and be leaving Red to be closer to his family.

Adam also proved his leadership as he kept the jackals and hyenas at bay. He did not allow them to take advantage of Seth's departure. Adam informed them and all the animals of Red that he was bringing in a new leader.

The new leader was going to be Daniel from the jungle of Blue . . .

Chapter 4

Daniel comes from Blue

Daniel was excited about the chance to rule his own jungle. He was a rather young lion who was aggressive, energetic and strong. He had been in line for the leadership position in Blue for a few years now. However, he would have had to wait many more years for the chance to take over there. He had been frustrated by the wait and had been considering leaving Rainbow for other possible opportunities. He had even spent time talking with Adam about his possible move out of Rainbow.

Adam had hoped to find a suitable place for Daniel so that Rainbow would not lose this dynamic young leader. Now Adam could offer something real that might fit Daniel's needs and potential. Daniel accepted Adam's offer and quickly moved to Red with his family. Once Daniel got there, Adam left to take care of his other responsibilities in Rainbow.

After they got settled, Daniel talked to Lulu, his wife, about his ideas, worries and plans for Red. While he never asked me, Opal, for advice, I heard all their conversations. After all, an owl listens all the time.

Excited about his chance to lead, Daniel quickly decided that Red's local animals didn't fit in with his style of leadership. They couldn't meet his expectations for performance and he didn't understand their local way of doing things.

So, he decided to bring in a team of young lions from Blue. After all, he'd known them as young cubs and felt comfortable with them. He claimed that lions were the best animals in the jungle; they were the kings.

The local animals were offended and saddened by the lack of respect for local talent. Daniel hadn't even given them a chance to show what they could do. He didn't ask for advice and didn't respect the opinions or ideas of those with many years of experience in Red.

I watched all kinds of chaos occur. The young lions from Blue roared in and started ordering changes that were not needed. They began correcting the alligators about patrolling the river crossings. The spiders got all tangled up when following the lions' web design directions. The giraffes began to complain about neck injuries from eating lower level vegetation. The direct and disrespectful young lions made everyone miserable and rebellious.

Then, the young lions on Daniel's imported team began to fight among themselves. They couldn't agree on what to do or how to do things. They just couldn't get things done right. They blamed the animals of Red for their problems. Then they blamed each other. Furthermore they blamed Daniel for their problems and their inability to be successful. All this took place behind Daniel's back. And Daniel's wife, Lulu, began to bad-mouth Red.

The animals of Red became disgruntled and could not get on with their jobs. When word got back to Adam, he traveled to Red once again. He now had the unpleasant task of sending Daniel and Lulu packing. Daniel had to be told that his performance wasn't satisfactory, and that his team was ineffective and had to go.

They didn't go quietly, especially Daniel and Lulu. When he heard about the impending change in his leadership position, Daniel charged into the office. He was embarrassed because he had to tell his whole team that they were leaving with him. And he placed the blame for his lack of success on Adam. Daniel said that Adam hadn't given him enough support or time to be successful.

Adam was appalled with the drama that Daniel tried to create at the office. Then Lulu added to this by confronting Adam and accusing him of ruining their lives. The other lions growled and grumbled menacingly as they packed and left.

Now Adam had to find another leader for Red and he needed one immediately. So, Adam sent for Quentin . . .

Chapter 5

Quentin arrives from Yellow

Quentin had an excellent reputation and performance record. He was the eagle who had led the desert community of Yellow. Under his leadership, Yellow had prospered and the animals all worked well together. But there was no real challenge left for Quentin there.

Adam knew this and thought Quentin was ready for the new challenge that Red would present. Quentin was excited about the opportunities Red might offer. He saw this leadership assignment as a stepping-stone to his next promotion. He hoped to one day have Adam's position as leader of Rainbow.

Once Quentin got to Red, he began to take control of the situation. Quentin did come to me, Opal, and tell me his plans. I guess he felt comfortable confiding in another bird. But he never asked for my opinions or advice.

Quentin decided to make changes in everyone's job assignments. As a result, animals from Red were given new and unusual tasks that they weren't equipped to do. For example, the pythons were required to carry rattles while the leopards were told to change their spots. These changes didn't work well at all and everyone complained. Quentin felt the need for reinforcements.

A few days later, we started to see a very strange group of desert animals arriving to take up their roles. Some of these animals were rattlesnakes, turkey vultures, camels, Gila monsters, scorpions, toads and jackrabbits. It seemed that Quentin had decided to change Red into another Yellow. He felt comfortable with the animals and environment of Yellow. After all, he had been successful there, so he apparently thought that what had worked in Yellow should work in Red.

These animals had many problems trying to live in Red. They were used to living in the desert of Yellow and couldn't adapt to our Red jungle conditions. So they then tried to change the jungle into something more akin to their Yellow desert. Trees fell, grasses were cut, holes were dug, and the jungle became a disaster area.

Not only was the environment being ruined but conflict erupted among the animals and even became physical. I saw Hector, the hyena, fighting over scraps with Tomas, the turkey vulture. Irene, the impala, broke a leg in a jackrabbit hole that had been ordered dug in the middle of the main path.

Once again, chaos reigned. Something had to be done to restore harmony and the jungle. Word was again sent to Adam about the situation. When he arrived he realized that Quentin and his desert team would have to go. They were just not right for Red. This time, the desert team left quietly because all were so uncomfortable in Red.

Later, I overheard Adam talking to himself as he considered what to do next. He knew that another mistake would ruin his reputation as he neared the end of his career. He realized that another set of outside lions or desert animals wouldn't be the answer. So he decided to step in and rule Red himself.

I thought it would be interesting to watch how effective Adam would be as Red's leader . . .

Chapter 6

Adam steps in

Red needed a firm hand and strong leadership to bring it back in line after the series of mismatches between leadership and the Red community. Adam proved to be the strong, firm hand that was needed.

His hands-on leadership got things back on track. The impalas were doing their work; the alligators were patrolling the rivers; the trees were growing in the right places; the holes (that the jackrabbits from Yellow had dug) were filled. Daily operations were moving ahead smoothly. Moreover, all the different animals in the community of Red were happy once again.

However, while everything was going well in Red, other problems loomed on the horizon for Adam. In his effort to turn Red around, he'd been neglecting his duties as the leader of Rainbow. In addition he hadn't been able to give the desert community of Yellow and the other jungle community of Blue any real attention.

Both Yellow and Blue began to complain that they were being ignored. Their problems were going unheeded, and their needs for advice and guidance were not being met. Adam had been neglecting the greater overall needs of Rainbow, and as its leader, was also neglecting his other responsibilities.

Adam began to recognize that his real responsibility to Red was to find a good leader, not to be one. After all, he had progressed beyond the Red level of leadership.

As I, Opal, kept watch, I saw Adam change and become a different leader and lion. He was probably homesick for his family and his own den. He also knew that he wasn't doing the best he could for all. He felt a lot of pressure to find a good leader for Red and get back to his duties at Rainbow headquarters.

And because he was lonely, stressed and unhappy, I saw Adam's behavior change. He started hanging out with the hyenas at night, especially their leader, Hector . . .

Chapter 7

Hector makes a move

I watched Hector, the hyena leader, close in on Adam. Hector sensed that Adam was vulnerable.

Adam was far from home, and alone in Red without any personal support. Hector saw this as his opportunity to build his own case for taking charge of Red.

Hector made sure that Adam always had a hyena available to help out. Hector also ensured that his hyenas kept all the other animals at bay. Even though the other animals wanted to help Adam, they couldn't get near him.

In addition, Hector and his hyenas started to become Adam's social circle. They all went out nights together. They tried to change Adam's habits to theirs. And Hector started to fill Adam's ear with Hector's version of the truth about Red.

I also heard Hector giving Adam advice about who to select as the next leader of Red. His suggestion was himself, Hector.

When I heard this, I could no longer remain silent. I knew it was time for me, Opal, to speak out . . .

Chapter 8

Opal opens up

When I heard Hector trying to manipulate and take control of the leadership of Red, I was appalled. I knew that as a Red resident and a wise old owl, I had to speak up. I only hoped that I wasn't too late and that Adam would listen to me. I was afraid that even if he listened to me, he might not heed my advice.

It was difficult to get Adam alone and away from the hyenas. However, once I did, I found Adam to be very level-headed and receptive. He heard me out as I described his personal and regional responsibilities as the leader of the country of Rainbow. I was also able to make him see how Hector and his gang of hyenas were manipulating the situation.

Adam shared his sense of loneliness with me. He explained that he missed his own family and home den. He told me that he felt frustrated because he knew that he should be taking care of all the other problems in Rainbow. But, he felt trapped into focusing only on the local needs of the jungle of Red because he couldn't identify a suitable leader who could do the job.

As we talked, Adam confided to me that the only resident animal who had voiced an interest in becoming the leader of Red had been Hector. I let him know that Hector was not making it easy for Adam to talk to and get to know the other animals of Red. We spent a long time talking about Hector's real and imagined qualifications. I shared my observations and what I felt were the community opinions of Hector as a hyena leader and Red community member.

I was very careful about speaking too strongly or negatively about Hector. I didn't want to lose Adam's trust and openness to our conversation. I avoided telling Adam that all the animals had no respect for Hector as a community member, and that they were offended by his hygiene issues such as body odor and bad breath.

Adam seemed to accept the evaluation of Hector. He agreed that Hector was probably not the right animal for the Red leader position. And then he asked me, Opal, to suggest someone who was suitable.

I'd been thinking about this ever since Seth had retired. I'd also been talking to all the other animals about their ideas for a suitable Red leader to replace Seth the lion. As we saw the imported leaders try, stumble and fail, we knew we needed someone local. The right leader for Red would probably be someone who was local, intelligent, culturally sensitive, decisive, firm, fair and respected.

When Adam asked who fit that description, I answered, "Edgar . . ."

Chapter 9

Edgar is selected

"But Edgar is an elephant!" said Adam. "Leaders are lions."

I countered that not all lions are leaders and that not all leaders have to be lions. It was only a jungle tradition. However, the other animals weren't always happy with lions as leaders, especially when a better qualified animal was available.

Furthermore, I reminded Adam that not only had he brought in Quentin, the eagle, but he had been considering Hector, the hyena, as Red's next leader. Adam had again been on the verge of possibly choosing another non-lion to try to lead Red.

With that, Adam and I discussed Edgar and his qualifications one more time. Adam agreed to sleep on the idea. He would talk to members of the Red community the following morning to get their input and ideas.

As a result, Adam set up a meeting with Edgar the elephant. After speaking with Edgar, reviewing his qualifications and hearing the recommendations of the community, Adam offered Edgar the chance to assume the leadership of Red.

As Edgar stepped into his role as leader of Red, Adam bid me farewell and returned to his home and responsibilities of leading Rainbow. Adam promised to return in a few months to see how things were progressing. He left Edgar with his offer of support should it be needed in Red.

One of Edgar's first decisions was to build a strong team to lead the jungle of Red. His first addition to the team was me, Opal, the owl, and we worked together to build the best team for Red that we could. We agreed that Red needed a diverse leadership team of qualified animals. This would help Edgar gain the respect of all the animals in the community of Red.

I also suggested that Edgar consider the future needs of Red. To do this, it would be wise to grow the next leader so that Red and Rainbow could avoid the problems we had been facing since Seth's departure.

Edgar agreed and suggested Willie as his potential successor and second in command. I agreed as I knew Willie well.

Adam returned a few months later . . .

Chapter 10

Edgar and Willie team up

When Adam, our regional leader, returned a few months later, he was pleased. All of the operations in Red were running smoothly. Red was meeting its goals and responsibilities within Rainbow, and morale was high. Even Hector was toeing the line and doing his job.

Edgar the elephant was making good decisions as Red's leader. Even when the decisions were tough or unpopular, everyone understood and respected his strength. Although Edgar wasn't a lion, he was a true leader.

Adam and Edgar got together with me, Opal. Edgar invited me to talk with them about the changes that had taken place and his plans for the future. I made sure that Adam understood how Edgar had stepped up and done a wonderful job of getting Red moving forward. Adam agreed that all he had heard were good things about Edgar and the condition of the Red community. Adam was pleased to see how Edgar had taken control and was successfully leading Red.

When Adam asked about the future, Edgar started to speak up. He explained that many of Red's past problems had their roots in a lack of planned action for the future. One key issue that hadn't been addressed before was identifying and developing future leaders for Red.

Edgar had made this his top priority. But before he decided who that might be, Edgar had asked for input from many different animals on his team, including me, Opal, a wise owl. I let Adam know that I agreed with the general consensus and Edgar's final selection.

Edgar and I had discussed all the qualifications of the successful candidate. Edgar's choice was clearly the best animal for the job, head and shoulders above all the other possible and previous leaders. This candidate might even be better qualified than Edgar himself.

Edgar then told Adam that he had chosen Willie, the water buffalo, as the leader-in-training. Adam almost fainted.

"A water buffalo!" Adam roared in surprise.

"Yes, of course. Remember, Adam, there's no guarantee that any one animal is the best leader. Let's face it, you took a chance on me, an elephant," said Edgar. "Let me introduce you to Willie. You never had the chance to meet Willie when you were here before."

When Adam recovered from the shock of the suggestion, we went over to Willie's office. When we got there, Willie came out from behind her desk and greeted Adam. "Hello, my name is Wilhelmina, but everyone calls me Willie."

I thought Adam would have a cow. Adam's eyes just about popped out of his head as he turned to Edgar and said, "But . . . Willie is a girl!"

Edgar's response was so calm and typical of our leader, the elephant, "And your point is? She may be female but she has all the right qualifications and everyone's respect. What more do you need?"

I was proud of Adam. He took a second to compose himself and then greeted Willie very professionally.

Later Adam and I went off for a chat. He looked rather shaken and tired. I waited for him to say something.

He finally said, "You know, Opal, I think I am getting too old for this job. Things are changing too fast for me. I know Edgar and Willie are the right choices to lead Red. Maybe it's time for me to rethink my priorities."

A few months later, I, Opal, received a postcard from Adam, the lion . . .

Chapter 11

Opal's Epilogue

Adam's postcard shared some interesting new things with me.

After he'd left Red, Adam, the lion, had done some soul searching. He had thought about where he was in his life and career. He had discovered he really didn't want to continue as the regional leader of Rainbow.

He wanted to let me know his new address. He was moving to the Florida Everglades to retire and live near his cousin, Peter, the panther.

He also asked me to give Willie and Edgar his best wishes and to tell them about his new address. Adam's only request was that I, Opal, the owl, continue to share my wisdom and this story with anyone willing to listen . . .

—The End—